KU-176-232

Rough Guides

25 Ultimate experiences

Europe

Make the most of your time on Earth

ROUGH GUIDES

25 YEARS 1982–2007

NEW YORK • LONDON • DELHI

Contents

Introduction

EXPERIENCES have always been at the heart of the Rough Guide concept. A group of us began writing the books **25 years ago** (hence this celebratory mini series) and wanted to share the kind of travels we had been doing ourselves. It seems bizarre to recall that in the early 1980s, travel was very much a minority pursuit. Sure, there was a lot of tourism around, and that was reflected in the guidebooks in print, which traipsed around the established sights with scarcely a backward look at the local population and their life. We wanted to change all that: to put a country or a city's popular culture centre stage, to highlight the clubs where you could hear local music, drink with people you hadn't come on holiday with, watch the local football, join in with the festivals. And of course we wanted to push travel a bit further, inspire readers with the confidence and knowledge to break away from established routes, to find pleasure and excitement in remote islands, or desert routes, or mountain treks, or in street culture.

Twenty-five years on, that thinking seems pretty obvious: we all want to experience something real about a destination, and to seek out travel's **ultimate experiences**. Which is exactly where these **25 books** come in. They are not in any sense a new series of guidebooks. We're happy with the series that we already have in print. Instead, the **25s** are a collection of ideas, enthusiasms and inspirations: a selection of the very best things to see or do – and not just before you die, but now. Each selection is gold dust. That's the brief to our writers: there is no room here for the average, no space fillers. Pick any one of our selections and you will enrich your travelling life.

But first of all, take the time to browse. Grab a half dozen of these books and let the ideas percolate … and then begin making your plans.

Mark Ellingham
Founder & Series Editor, Rough Guides

25 Ultimate experiences
Europe

Canoeing down the DORDOGNE

Have you ever fancied paddling in speckled sunlight past ancient châteaux and honey-hued villages, stopping off for a spot of gentle sightseeing and ending the day with a well-earned gastronomic extravaganza? If so, then canoeing down the Dordogne river of southwest France is just the ticket.

need to know

Numerous canoe rental companies set up along the Dordogne in summer offering rental by the day or half-day. Some also offer longer excursions, including transport, tents and waterproof containers. The river is at its busiest during July and August.

For a 170-kilometre stretch from Argentat down to Mauzac the river provides classic canoeing. The scenery is glorious and varied, there are umpteen first-class sights within a stone's throw of the water and the choice of accommodation ranges from convivial campsites to rustic, village inns and luxury hotels in converted châteaux. The free-flowing river also offers a variety of canoeing conditions to suit beginners upwards, and though it's hardly white-water rafting, some of the Dordogne's rapids are sufficiently challenging, particularly in spring and early summer, to give at least a frisson of excitement.

Keen canoeists should start at Argentat, from where it takes roughly ten days to paddle downstream. The river here is fast, fun and more or less crowd-free. Beyond Beaulieu the current eases back as the river widens, and the first limestone outcrops and sandy beaches – perfect for a picnic lunch – start to appear. Souillac marks the beginning of the most famous – and busiest – stretch of river. If you can only spare one day, then paddle from Souillac, or Domme, to Beynac where the river loops beneath beetling cliffs from which medieval fortresses keep watch from their dizzying eyries. At water level you glide past walnut orchards, duck farms and houses drenched in geraniums.

The crowds fall behind as you slip past Beynac. There are fewer sights and the scenery is more mellow, though the Dordogne has one final treat in store at Limeuil as it writhes in two great meanders across the floodplain. Leave your canoe behind and head for the limestone cliffs for a bird's-eye view of this classic Dordogne scene.

A faint glimmer of flame behind the altar of the darkened church and the black-clad papás appears, holding aloft a lighted taper and chanting "*Avto to Fos*" – This is the Light of the World. Thus Easter Sunday begins at the stroke of midnight in a tiny chapel in Loutró, southern Crete. Minutes earlier, the congregation and entire village had been plunged into darkness. Now, as the priest ignites the first candle and the flame is passed from neighbour to neighbour, light spreads again throughout the church. As the congregation pours out into the street the candlelight is distributed to every home along with the cry of "*Christos Anesti*" (Christ is Risen). It's an extraordinary experience – a symbolic reawakening of brightness and hope with clear echoes of more ancient rites of spring – and within minutes wilder celebrations begin; firecrackers are thrown and traditional dishes devoured to break the week-long fast that the more devout have observed.

The rituals of the Greek Orthodox church permeate every aspect of Greek society, but never so clearly as at Easter. As a visitor you are inevitably drawn in, especially in a place as small as Loutró – accessible only by boat or on foot – where the locals go out of their way to include you.

After a few hours' sleep you wake to the smell of lambs and goats roasting on spits. As they cook, the wine and beer flow freely until the whole village, locals and visitors alike, join the great feasts to mark the end of Lent.

This is the Light:
Easter celebrations in Loutró

In towns and villages throughout Greece you can attend midnight mass and often be invited to the Bacchanalian feast of roast lamb the next day. There are particularly well-known celebrations on the islands of Crete, Ídhra, Corfu and Pátmos, but thousands of Greeks head to these places, and ferries and accommodation will be very busy; book well in advance

03

FJORD FOCUS:
touring
western Norway

Everything about the Geirangerfjord is dramatic, even the approach: zigzagging up the through the mountains from Ändalsnes before throwing yourself round a series of hair-raising bends as you descend the aptly named Ørnevegen, or Eagle's Highway, the fjord glittering like a precious gem below.

need to know

Geirangerfjord is in southwestern Norway, 9hr by bus from Bergen, or 17hr 45min via Åndalsnes and the Trollstigen. Norddalsfjord is 45min to the north; the other fjords are much closer to Bergen: Naerøyfjord (3hr) and Lustrafjord (5hr). You'll get more out of the western fjords if you rent a car.

The Geirangerfjord, a great slice of deep blue carved into the crystalline rock walls and snaking out an "S" shape as it weaves west, is one of the region's smallest fjords – but also one of its most beautiful. From the pretty little village that marks its eastern end, ferries set out on the sixteen-kilometre trip along the fjord west to Hellesylt. On a summer's day, as the ferry eases away from the wooden pier and chugs off slowly through the passage, waterfalls cascading down the sheer walls on either side and dolphins playing in the bow waves – as they have done since the first cruise ship found its way up here in 1869 – it's easy to see why UNESCO considered this to be the archetypal fjord, recently awarding it World Heritage status.

As beautiful as it is, Geirangerfjord is just one sliver of water in a network of stunning strands, and you need to see a few fjords to appreciate their magnificence as a whole. Head south for Naerøyfjord, the narrowest fjord in the world, where you can savour the emerald green waters close up, in a kayak. Or hop in the car and glide across on a tiny ferry, over nearby Norddalsfjord, or – to the south – glass-like Lustrafjord, the wind whipping off the water as you stand at the very mouth of the boat, the imposing silhouette of Urnes' Viking stave church looming ever closer.

04 Taking a trip on the Moscow metro

After a few vodkas my Russian neighbour unfailingly produces the two English phrases he learned in his Soviet childhood. One concerns friendship between nations, the other, that the Moscow metro is the greatest in the world.

This second assertion isn't far from the truth. The Moscow metro was designed as an eighth wonder of the world, a great egalitarian art gallery for the proletariat, combining utility and beauty as it ferried workers around the city, beguiled them with sculpture and chandeliers and indoctrinated them with Soviet propaganda. Even now, it's hard not to believe, just a little bit, in the Soviet dream when you step out of a clean, quick underground train (one every two minutes) into the fabulously ornate stations. Perhaps that's why hard-bitten Muscovites never seem to raise their eyes from their hurrying feet, and it's easy to spot the tourists.

With twelve lines and over 170 stations, the problem is where to start exploring. The Koltsevaya, or ring, is the most distinctive and navigable metro line. Built in the 1950s, its twelve stops include some of the finest stations, and as it's a circular line, it's hard to get lost. Park Kultury was the first station to be built on the line, and is decorated with bas-reliefs of workers enjoying sports and dancing. Travelling anti-clockwise, pretty, white and sky-blue Taganskaya is a mere prelude to Komsomolskaya, one of the most awesome stations on the whole system. Komsomolskaya connects to railway terminals for St Petersburg and Siberia, and the vast chandeliers suspended from an opulent baroque ceiling are designed to impress newly arrived travellers.

Towards the end of the circuit, Novoslobodskaya is the loveliest station of all. In the light of its jewel-bright stained-glass panels, even infamously surly Muscovites seem to smile and, recalling my Russian neighbour's English phrases, you may even start believing in friendship between nations. Which takes us neatly to Kievskaya, adorned with mosaic depictions of historical events uniting Russia and Ukraine, and the last stop on your circular journey.

need to know

Open daily 6am–1am. Adult tickets cost 15 roubles (about €0.50) – valid throughout the entire metro.

05

Hogmanay:
bringing in the New Year
Scottish style

Like all the best celebrations,
Hogmanay has its feet firmly planted
in the pagan past. A traditional
festival of hedonistic misrule, it's
designed to blast away the mid-
winter blues and is celebrated with
passionate intensity in Scotland,
from the borders to the farthest flung
islands.

need to know

Tickets for Hogmanay in Edinburgh are available
from October from the Hub on Castlehill
(☎0131/473 2000, ☻www.thehub-edinburgh.
com). For great live music and some dancing,
head north to the **Ceilidh Place** in Ullapool
(☎01854/612 103, ☻www.theceilidhplace.com).

Though the general idea is now a miasma of drunkenness topped off with some fireworks, the festival as it is celebrated in Scotland has some very particular customs. It is traditionally a time to settle your affairs, and then welcome luck into your home by first footing – visiting your neighbours with gifts, originally a lump of coal. The luckiest visitor is considered to be a tall, dark-haired man, perhaps for obvious reasons.

Even the smallest village will host some sort of Hogmanay celebration – while these can be of a churningly sentimental tartan nature, you can also get lucky and hear great live music. A good option is to find a genuine ceilidh, where musicians improvise around standard folk songs, often to wild,

exhilarating effect. And nothing will help you shed your inhibitions like a bit of Scottish country dancing – a caller shouts instructions, but taking a wrong turn in an eightsome reel is half the fun.

Scotland's major Hogmanay magnet, though, is the city of Edinburgh, where the once chaotic celebrations have been transformed into a major ticketed event, with bands, dancing and 100,000 people on the streets. The bells at midnight are the signal to start the fireworks, the floodlit castle and the jagged silhouette of the old town providing the most dramatic of backdrops. At this point strangers will grab your hands, pump your arms up and down, and bellow out Auld Lang Syne, and any last shreds of Scottish Presbyterian reserve are abandoned.

VI

The Colosseum

IN WINTER

Is there a more recognizable architectural profile in existence? Featured on everything from Olympic medals to Italy's five euro coin, the Colosseum has been the model for just about every stadium built since. Even our word "arena" derives from the Latin word for sand, which was used to soak up the blood of the unfortunate gladiators and various beasts who died here.

The Colosseum wasn't good enough for the film director Ridley Scott, who regarded it as too small for the film *Gladiator* and had a larger replica mocked up in Malta instead. But for the rest of the world it does nicely as a reminder of the cruelty and brutality of the Roman world, home as it was to its gladiatorial games and the ritual slaughter of exotic animals by the ton; the emperor Trajan was perhaps the most bloodthirsty ruler to raise his thumb here: his games of 108–109 AD consumed around 11,000 animals and involved 10,000 gladiators. The blood baths may have gone out of fashion, but the Colosseum's magnificent architecture is timeless. The Romans were not known for their diminutive constructions, but this is by far the largest building they produced – and probably its cleverest too, ingeniously designed so that its 60,000 spectators could exit in around twenty minutes.

Nowadays it's a bit of a Disneyland of kiss-me-quick gladiators and long queues, so it's better to visit out of season, preferably on a weekday as soon as it opens, when there's no one around. Coming here on a gloomy January morning may not have quite the same appeal as a sunny day in spring or summer, but wandering alone through the Colosseum's grand corridors and gazing down into its perfectly proportioned arena, gives you the chance to appreciate this seminal building at its best.

need to know
The Colosseum opens at 9am every day except Christmas Day and closes at 4.30pm between November and February; entry is €11.

I don't think he actually said "Mush! Mush!" – all I caught was a little click of the teeth and a high-pitched cry – but the dogs still howled and yapped and took off through the snow like hounds out of hell.

07
mush! mush!

Husky sledding in the Swiss Alps

need to know

Loschadej's Huskypower (June–Oct; ®www.huskypower.ch) operates on the Diablerets glacier, in southwestern Switzerland. A half-hour ride costs Sfr75/€45 per person.

We were up at 3000m, whisking across the snowfields on a sled drawn by eight huskies yoked in pairs. Earlier, the musher, René, had pointed out the different breeds to us – most were regular huskies, with their pale coats and blue eyes, but he also had several stocky, dark-pelted Greenlands. It was about ten degrees below freezing, under a crystal-clear blue sky – really too warm for them: these dogs prefer temperatures nearer minus thirty.

The sled was a simple affair, a couple of metres long, with a platform at the back for the musher to stand with reins in hand and us sitting below, facing the bobbing tails of the rearmost pair of dogs. We whooshed along: what a great way to travel! Human and dog working together, in a spectacular natural setting of high peaks and grand panoramas.

Even on that short ride, we could see the pack at work: René had yoked an adolescent trainee alongside one of the old matriarchs at the front, and she was doling out some training of her own, with the odd nip to keep the young'un in line.

As we arrived back at base, the rest of the pack set up a frantic howling to greet the returnees, who stood, tongues out, panting clouds of steamy breath. They looked fantastic – I wanted to set off again into the wilderness and never come back.

08

Watching the hurling at Croke Park, Dublin

The player leaps like a basketball star through a crowd of desperate opponents and flailing sticks. Barely visible to the naked eye, the arcing ball somehow lodges in his upstretched palm. Dropping to the ground, he shimmies his way out of trouble, the ball now delicately balanced on the flat end of his hurley, then bang! With a graceful, scything pull, he slots the ball through the narrow uprights, seventy yards away.

Such is the stuff of Irish boyhood dreams, an idealized sequence of hurling on continual rewind. With similarities to lacrosse and hockey – though it's not really like either – hurling is a thrilling mix of athleticism, timing, outrageous bravery and sublime skill. Said to be the fastest team game in the world, it can be readily enjoyed by anyone with an eye for sport.

The best place to watch a match is Croke Park, the headquarters of the GAA (Gaelic Athletic Association). In this magnificent, 80,000-seater stadium, you'll experience all the colour, banter and passion of inter-county rivalry. And before the game, you can visit the excellent GAA Museum to get up to speed on hurling and its younger brother, Gaelic football, ancient sports whose renaissance was entwined with the struggle for Irish independence. Here, you'll learn about the first Bloody Sunday in 1920, when British troops opened fire on a match at this very ground, killing twelve spectators and one of the players. You'll be introduced to the modern-day descendants of Cúchulain, the greatest warrior-hero of Irish mythology, who is said to have invented hurling: star players of the last century such as flat-capped Christy Ring of Cork and more recent icons such as Kilkenny's D.J. Carey. And finally, you can attempt to hit a hurling ball yourself – after a few fresh-air shots, you'll soon appreciate the intricate skills the game requires.

need to know

Croke Park and the GAA Museum are in north Dublin; for information about matches and museum entry go to @www. gaa.ie. Expect to pay €35 for a good seat at the All-Ireland hurling quarter-finals, for example.

Surely only a Spanish artist could generate the kind of public disturbance usually reserved for *La Liga*.

Opened in 1819 at the behest of Ferdinand VII, Madrid's El Prado has long been one of the world's premier art galleries, with vaults so vast only a fraction of the paintings can be exhibited at any one time. Among those treasures – gleaned largely from the salons of the Spanish nobility – are half of the complete works of Diego Velázquez, virtuoso court painter to Felipe IV. Such was the clamour surrounding a 1990 exhibition that half-a-million people filed through the turnstiles; those locked out clashed with civil guards. What Velázquez himself would've made of it all is hard to say; in his celebrated masterpiece *Las Meninas,* he peers out inscrutably from behind his own canvas, dissolving the boundaries between viewer and viewed, superimposing scene upon reflected scene.

Strung out over two floors, the works of Francisco de Goya are equally revolutionary, ranging from sybaritic portraiture to piercing documents of trauma both personal and political. It's difficult to imagine public disorder over his infamous *Pinturas Negras,* nor do they attract the spectatorial logjams of *Las Meninas,* yet they're not works you'll forget in a hurry. The terrible magnetism of paintings like *The Colossus* and *Saturn Devouring One of His* Sons is easier to comprehend in the context of their creation, as the last will and testament of a profoundly deaf and disillusioned old man, fearful of his own flight into madness. Originally daubed on the walls of his farmhouse, the black paintings take to extremes motifs that Goya had pioneered: *Tres de Mayo* is unflinching in depicting the tawdry horror of war, its faceless Napoleonic executioners firing a fusillade that echoes into the twenty-first century.

Portraits
and Purgatory:

Viewing Velázquez and Goya at the Prado

There's an indefinable
scent that, in an instant,
brings the Greek islands
vividly to mind. A mixture,
perhaps, of thyme-covered
slopes cooling overnight
and the more prosaic smells
of the port, of fish and
octopus, overlaid with the
diesel exhaust of the ferry
that's carrying you there.
A moment at night when
you can sense approaching
land but not yet see it, just
moonlight reflecting off the
black Aegean and sparkling
in the churning wake.

Travelling between the

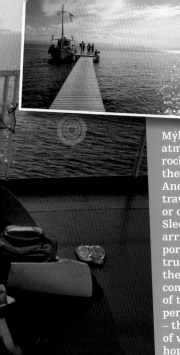

There are well over 1000 Greek islands, perhaps a tenth of them inhabited. Almost all of those have some kind of ferry connection, and no two are the same. From party islands like Íos or Mýkonos to the sober, monastic atmosphere of Pátmos, from tiny rocks to the vastness of Crete, there's an island for every mood. And there's a visceral thrill in travelling by sea that no plane or coach or car can ever match. Sleeping on deck under the stars; arriving in a rock-girt island port at dawn; chaos as cars and trucks and human cargo spill off the ship; black-clad old ladies competing to extol the virtues of their rooms. Clichéd images perhaps, but clichés for a reason – this is still one of the essentials of world travel, uniquely Greek, hopelessly romantic.

islands by boat, it feels like little has changed in hundreds of years. Dolphins really do still leap around the prow, days are stiflingly hot, nights starlit and glassy. The ferries may be modern but the old adventure stubbornly refuses to die.

How to do it

The starting point for almost all Greek island travels is Athens' port at Pireás. From here there are hundreds of daily departures in every direction. Except at Easter or the first two weeks of August, reservations are rarely necessary. Timetables change constantly, and are subject to the weather, so the only truly accurate information is at the port, on the day: simply turn up and buy a ticket.

11
HAVING A BEER IN BRUSSELS

Don't just ask for a beer in Belgium – your request will be met with a blank stare. Because no one produces such a wide range of beers as they do here: there are lagers, wheat beers, dark amber ales, strong beers brewed by Trappist monks, beers with fruit added, even beers mixed with grapes. Some beers are fermented in the cask, others in the bottle and corked champagne-like. And each beer has its own glass, specifically developed to enhance the enjoyment of that particular brew.

Brussels is the best place to try all of them, including its own beery speciality, Lambic, a flattish concoction that is brewed in open barrels and

fermented with the naturally occurring yeasts in the air of the Payottenland (the area around Brussels). It's not much changed from to the stuff they drank in Bruegel's time, and a few glasses is enough to have you behaving like one of the peasants in his paintings – something you can do to your heart's content at *La Becasse*, down an alley not far from the Grande-Place, or at the Cantillon Brewery in the Anderlecht district, where they still brew beer using these old methods, and which you can visit on regular tours.

You can taste another potent brew, Gueuze, a sparkling, cidery affair, at *La Mort Subite*, a dodgy-sounding name for a comfortable fin-de-siècle café; your ale will be served with brisk efficiency by one of the ancient staff, and while you sip it you can munch on cubes of cheese with celery salt or cold meats like jellied pigs cheeks. After this aperitif, make your way to *'t Spinnekopke*, a restaurant that cooks everything in beer, and has lots to drink as well, or just head for *Delirium*, a quarter of whose 2000-strong beer menu is Belgian. Finish up with a glass of Westvleteren brown ale, a Trappist brew that was recently voted the best beer in the world – and at 10.3 percent it's also one of the strongest.

need to know

La Becasse rue Tabora 11
Cantillon Brewery rue Gheude 67
La Mort Subite rue Montagne-aux-Herbes
  Potageres 7
't Spinnekopke Place Jardin aux Fleurs 1
Delirium Impasse de la Fidelité 4a

12

Getting hot and bothered

There's over half a million saunas in Finland – that's one for every ten Finns – and they have played an integral part in Finnish life for centuries. Finns believe the sauna to be an exorcism of all ills, and there's certainly nothing quite like it for inducing a feeling of serenity.

Always a single-sex affair, the sauna is a wonderfully levelling experience **since everybody is naked** (it's insisted upon for hygiene reasons). After first showering, take a paper towel or a small wooden tray and place this on one of the benches inside, arranged in the form of a gallery, before you sit down. This stops the benches from burning your skin. Traditionally a sauna is heated by a wood-burning stove which fills the room with a rich smell of wood smoke. However, more often than not today, saunas are electrically heated, typically to around 80–90°C, **a claustrophobic, lung-filling heat.** Ever so often, when the air gets too dry, water is thrown onto the hot stones that sit on top of the stove, which then hiss furiously and cause a blast of steam.

By this point you'll be sweating profusely, streams pouring off you and pooling on the ground, prompting the next stage in your sauna experience – lashing yourself with birch twigs. The best saunas provide bathers with small birch branches, with leaves still on, with which you **gently strike yourself** to increase blood circulation. The fresh smell of the birch in the hot air, coupled with the tingling feeling on the skin, is **wondrously sensual**. Traditionally Finns end their sauna by mercilessly plunging straight into the nearest lake or, in winter, by **rolling in the icy snow** outside – the intense searing cold that follows the sweltering heat creating a compelling, addictive rush at the boundary of pleasure and pain.

in Finland

need to know

Most public swimming pools in Finland have saunas. One of the best traditional saunas is Kotiharjun sauna (Tues–Fri 2–8pm, Sat 1–7pm) on Harjutorinkatu street in Helsinki.

13

Joining the *truffle* trail in Buzet, Istria

Even the most committed of culinary explorers often find the truffle to be something of an acquired taste. Part nutty, part mushroomy, part sweaty sock, the subtle but insistent flavour of this subterranean fungus nevertheless inspires something approaching gastronomic hysteria among its army of admirers.

need to know

The Buzet tourist office (☎385 52 662-343, ⌨www.buzet.hr) has details of the *Buzetska Subotina* festival, and can also direct you towards the best local restaurants.
Toklarija Sovinjsko polje ☎385 52 663-031
Vrh Vrh ☎385 52 667-123

Nowhere is truffle worship more fervent than in the Croatian province of Istria, a beautiful region where medieval hill towns sit above bottle-green forests. Summer is the season for the delicately flavoured white truffle, although it's the more pungent autumnal black truffle that will really bring out the gourmet in you. A few shavings of the stuff delicately sprinkled over pasta has an overpowering, lingering effect on your tastebuds.

The fungus-hunting season is marked by a plethora of animated rural festivals. Biggest of the lot is held in the normally sleepy town of Buzet, where virtually everyone who is anyone in Istria gathers on a mid-September weekend to celebrate the *Buzetska Subotina*, or "Buzet Saturday". As evening approaches, thousands of locals queue for a slice of the world's biggest truffle omelette, fried up in a mind-bogglingly large pan on the town's main square. With the evening rounded out with folk dancing, fireworks, al-fresco pop concerts and large quantities of *biska* – the local mistletoe-flavoured brandy – this is one small-town knees-up that no one forgets in a hurry.

Buzet's reputation as Istria's truffle capital has made this otherwise bland provincial town a magnet for in-the-know foodie travellers. The revered fungus plays a starring role in the dishes at *Toklarija*, a converted oil-pressing shed in the nearby hilltop settlement of Sovinjsko polje, whose head chef changes the menu nightly in accordance with what's fresh in the village. One of the best meals you're likely to eat is in the neighbouring hamlet of Vrh, where the family-run *Vrh* inn serves fat rolls of home-made pasta stuffed with truffles, mushrooms, asparagus and other locally gathered goodies. With the ubiquitous mistletoe brandy also on the menu, a warm glow of satisfaction is guaranteed.

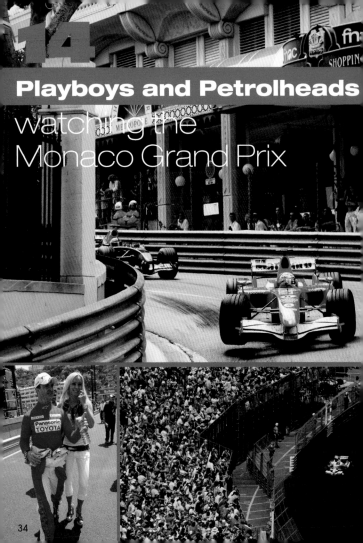

14

Playboys and Petrolheads

watching the
Monaco Grand Prix

From the **hotel-sized yachts** in the harbour to the celebrity-filled Casino, the Grand Prix in Monaco is more than a motor race – it's **a three day playboy paradise**. The Monaco crown is still the most sought after in motor-racing circles, although today's event is as much a showcase for the richest men and women on the planet as it is for the drivers.

Set amongst the winding streets of the world's second smallest and most densely populated principality, this is the most glamorous and high-profile date on the Formula One calendar. Attracting a global television audience of millions, the cars roar their way around the city centre at four-times the speed the streets were designed for. The circuit is blessed with some of the most historic and memorable corners in motor racing: **St Devote, Mirabeau, La Rascasse, Casino** and, of course, **the Tunnel**. Part of Monaco's appeal is its renowned difficulty. Three-times Formula One World Champion Nelson Piquet once described the tackling the circuit as like, "riding a bicycle around your living room."

Watching this gladiatorial spectacle around the **Portier corner** is particularly thrilling – one of the few possible, if unlikely, overtaking points on the course – seeing the cars' flaming exhausts before they disappear into the Tunnel, the deafening roar of the engines echoing behind. But one of the best and cheapest places to watch the race is the standing-only **Secteur Rocher**, a grassy area on a hill above the last corner – **Rascasse** – at the circuit's western end, which offers fine views and attracts the most passionate F1 supporters. The cars look pretty small from up here, but watching them sweep past is incredible. And afterwards you can climb down for a stroll or drive around the circuit, which is reopened to traffic every evening: just don't imagine you're Michael Schumacher – the normal speed limit still applies.

15

Catching the cultural zeitgeis in Graz

need to know

Graz Tourist Office
ⓦwww.graztourismus.at.
Kunsthaus Graz (Tues–Sun
10am–6pm;
ⓦwww.kunsthausgraz.at).
Neue Galerie (Tues–Sun 10am–
6pm; ⓦwww.neuegalerie.at).
Forum Stadtpark (Tues–Fri
10am–6pm, Sat & Sun 2–6pm;
ⓦwww.forum.mur.at).
The Styrian Autumn Festival
is held annually from late
September to mid-October.

Throughout 2006, when most of Austria was celebrating the 250th birthday of a baby-faced composer in a curly wig, visitors to the southern city of Graz were confronted with jumbo-sized posters declaring the area "a Mozart-free zone". Graz has good reason to get cheeky about Austria's heritage industry. In recent years this quaint Habsburg town has reinvented itself as a trendy twenty-first-century destination, thanks in large part to the Kunsthaus Graz, a landmark exhibition centre opened in 2003 to celebrate the city's one-year reign as European Capital of Culture.

Nicknamed the "friendly alien", the curvy Kunsthaus billows up above the city's baroque buildings like the back of a leaping urban whale. Resembling the cargo hold of an interplanetary spacecraft, the interior could easily double as the set for one of local boy Arnold Schwarzenegger's sci-fi movies. It's certainly well suited to the ground-breaking art exhibitions that have established the Kunsthaus as a must-visit destination for anyone interested in central European art.

After stroking your chin at the Kunsthaus, you can cross the river Mur to check out yet more contemporary exhibitions at the Neue Galerie, before striding uphill to see what's going on at the Forum Stadtpark, a bunker-like gallery in the city park which has been a major focus of mad-cap cultural happenings since the 1960s.

Graz is also famous for being the host city of the Steierischer Herbst (Styrian autumn), one of Europe's most delightfully baffling festivals of contemporary art, music and new media. Visit while its on and not only will you collide with crowds of culture-freaks but you'll also be able to join in celebrations of Styria's pumpkin harvest. The love lavished on this locally grown vegetable is another addition to the city's growing armoury of eccentricities.

Tivoli's *fairground* attractions

Not many cities have a rollercoaster, a pirate ship and an 80-metre-high carousel slap bang in their centre, but Copenhagen is home to Tivoli – probably the best fairground in the world. The famous pleasure gardens have dished out fun and thrills to a bewitched public since 1843 – to the deeply patriotic Danes they're a national treasure, while most foreign visitors are lured through the gates by the charming mix of old and new: pretty landscaped gardens, fairground stalls, pantomime theatres and old-fashioned rickety rides rub shoulders with brash, high-octane newcomers like the Golden Tower, which will have you plunging vertically from a height of 60m, and the Demon – a stomach-churning three-loop rollercoaster.

need to know

Tivoli (@www.tivoli.dk) is a stone's throw from the main train station. The summer season runs from the mid-April to mid-September. It's also open for one week in mid-October and for the Christmas season (mid-Nov to end Dec). Tickets cost 75kr (€10) for adults, 35kr (€5) for children (ages 3–11), then 15–60kr (€2–8) per ride or multi-ride day tickets are 200kr (€27) for adults, 150kr (€20) for children. Expect to pay around twenty percent more for your food inside the park; prices for alcoholic drinks are a white-knuckle ride in themselves.

But the rides are just the icing on the cake – whether you're grabbing a hot dog or candy floss from the fast-food stands, or splashing out in one of the thirty or so restaurants, eating is also part of the Tivoli experience. Music plays a big role too, be it jazz and blues in the bandstands, Friday night rock on the open-air stage or the more stellar offerings of Tivoli Koncertshal, with its big name international acts – anyone from Anne-Sophie Mutter to Beck. In October, the whole place is festooned with pumpkins, ghouls and witches for a Halloween-themed extravaganza, and in the weeks around Christmas, the festive spirit is cranked up with spectacular lighting displays, a "Christmas Market", a skating rink by the Chinese pagoda and all sorts of tasty Christmas nibbles and warming *glögg*, while the braziers and torches help keep the worst of the Danish winter at bay.

Even if fairs usually leave you cold, you can't fail to be won over by the innocent pleasures of Tivoli. On a fine summer's night, with the twinkling illuminations, music drifting across the flowerbeds and fireworks exploding overhead, it's nothing short of magical.

Independence Street:
A night out in Istanbul's European heart

You've had a day or two's heavy sightseeing in Istanbul's Sultanahmet. You're culturally replete – but have a nagging feeling that you've missed something: the locals – just what the hell do they do in this metropolis of fifteen million souls? To find out, head across the Golden Horn to Independence Street (Istiklal Caddesi), the nation's liveliest thoroughfare.

need to know
From Sultanahmet take a tram to Karaköy then the Tünel funicular railway to the bottom of Independence Street; both close at 9pm. Return to Sultanahmet by taxi (around 20YTL/€11 after midnight). Information and tickets for events at venues around Istiklal Caddesi are available from @www.biletix.com

Lined with nineteenth-century apartment blocks and churches, and with a cute red turn-of-the-twentieth-century tramway, it was the fashionable centre of Istanbul's European quarter before independence, and it is now where young Istanbulites (and it's the youngest population of any European city) come to shop, eat, drink, take in a film, club, gig and gawk, 24/7.

the Turks are great talkers – wonderful meze, fish and lethal *raki* (akin to Greek ouzo). Later, blues, jazz and rock venues, pubs and trendy clubs burst into life – with the streets even busier than in daylight hours. You won't see many head-scarved woman here, and the call to prayer will be drowned by thumping western sounds. But though Islam may

By day, bare-shouldered Turkish girls in Benetton vests, miniskirts and Converse Allstars mingle with Armani-clad businessmen riding the city's financial boom, and music stores and fashion boutiques blare out the latest club sounds onto the shopper-thronged street. At night the alleyways off the main drag come to life. Cheerful tavernas serve noisy diners – and

have lost its grip on Istanbul's westernized youth, traditional Turkish hospitality survives even on Independence Street, and you may find yourself being offered a free beer or two. This is Istanbul's "happening" European heart, no wonder *Newsweek* heralded the city "Cool Istanbul: Europe's Hippest City".

EXPLORING MYSTICAL
Sintra

Inspiration for a host of writers – including Lord Byron and William Beckford – Sintra, the former summer retreat of Portuguese monarchs, is a town dotted with palaces and mansions, and surrounded by a series of wooded ravines. Now one or Europe's finest UNESCO World Heritage sites, Sintra has been a centre for cult worship for centuries: the early Celts named it Mountain of the Moon after one of their gods, and the hills are scattered with ley lines and mysterious tombs. Locals say batteries drain noticeably faster here and light bulbs pop with monotonous regularity.

Some claim it is because of the angle of iron in the rocks, others that it is all part of the mystical powers that lurk in Sintra's hills and valleys. There are certainly plenty of geographical and meteorological quirks: house-sized boulders litter the landscape as if thrown by giants, while a white cloud – affectionately known as the queen's fart – regularly hovers over Sintra's palaces even on the clearest summer day.

The fairytale palace of Palácio da Pena on the heights above town, with its dizzy views over the surrounding woodlands, looks like something

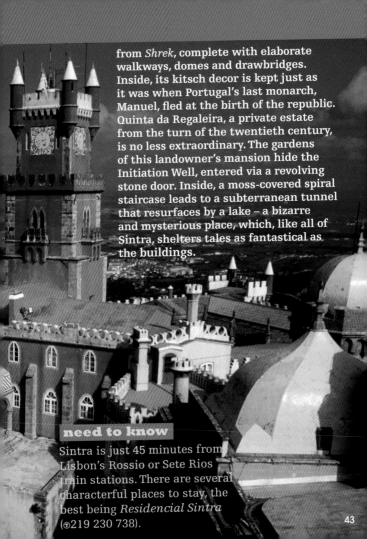

from *Shrek*, complete with elaborate walkways, domes and drawbridges. Inside, its kitsch decor is kept just as it was when Portugal's last monarch, Manuel, fled at the birth of the republic. Quinta da Regaleira, a private estate from the turn of the twentieth century, is no less extraordinary. The gardens of this landowner's mansion hide the Initiation Well, entered via a revolving stone door. Inside, a moss-covered spiral staircase leads to a subterranean tunnel that resurfaces by a lake – a bizarre and mysterious place, which, like all of Sintra, shelters tales as fantastical as the buildings.

need to know

Sintra is just 45 minutes from Lisbon's Rossio or Sete Rios train stations. There are several characterful places to stay, the best being *Residencial Sintra* (☎219 230 738).

19

Art after dark:
an evening in the Louvre

*I*f getting up close to the *Mona Lisa* was never easy, in the wake of *Da Vinci Code* fever it's now almost as challenging as the puzzle at the heart of Dan Brown's blockbuster, as you jostle for space with visitors plugged into Da Vinci audioguides pinpointing the grisly last movements of curator Jacques Saunière as described in the book's opening scenes.

However, come on a Wednesday or Friday evening for one of the Louvre's late openings, and you should find things much quieter; you'll also experience something of that "after dark" thrill as you wander the shadowy, labyrinthine corridors and catch glimpses through the windows of the atmospherically lit Classical facades.

need to know
The Louvre is open daily except Tuesday from 9am to 6pm; the "nocturnes" are 6–9.45pm on Wednesdays and Fridays. Tickets cost €8.50, €6 after 6pm.

If you can resist the general rush to the great Italian painting collection, follow signs instead to the lesser-visited Sully wing and seek out some of the rooms that date from the time when the Louvre was a palace not a museum. Enter the sumptuous Galerie d'Apollon and you'll feel you've stumbled upon some hidden treasure chamber: the extravagant gold decor gleams eerily in the semidarkness and a glittering case containing the crown jewels of France lures you to the far end. From here you could explore the peerless collection of Greek and Egyptian antiquities, or strike off into the enormous Richelieu wing and admire works by the Dutch masters Vermeer, Rembrandt and Rubens, or the towering giants of French art Ingres, David and Delacroix.

For most visitors though it is the outstanding Italian collection that exerts the biggest pull, and with good reason. The famous Grande Galerie, its blonde parquet stretching into the distance, displays all the great names in Italian Renaissance art: Mantegna, Botticelli, Titian, Bellini, Raphael, Veronese. And then of course there's Leonardo's *Mona Lisa*, propelled to fame when it was stolen in 1911. Like the *Da Vinci Code*'s character Sophie Neveu, who finds the painting "too little" and "foggy", you may well wonder at first what all the fuss is about, but if you can get close enough and overcome your own familiarity with the image, you might just find a strange and beguiling painting.

Ancient Aspendos

It's a hot summer's evening; overhead is a soft, purple-black and star strewn sky. There's the incessant chirrup of cicadas, mingled with the murmur of thousands of voices – Turkish, German, English, Russian – and the popping of corks, as the 15,000-strong audience settles down, passes round wine and olives and eagerly awaits the entertainment ahead. All are perched on hard, solid marble, still warm from the heat of the day, but the discomfort is a small price to pay to experience what a Roman citizen would have 1800 years ago, when this theatre, the largest and best preserved in Asia Minor, was built.

watching a live performance in a Roman amphitheatre

The views from the semi-circular auditorium, comprising forty tiers cut into the hillside, are magnificent. At sunset, the fading light on the remains of this once wealthy and powerful city and the Pamphylian plain beyond shows it at its best. There's a faint taste of the nearby Mediterranean on the breeze and the Taurus range in splendid silhouette to the north.

The stage lights play across the facade of the multi-level stage building, ornamented with Ionic and Corinthian columns, niches that once sported marble statues and elaborate friezes and pediments. The lights dim and the massed ranks of spectators fall silent. Slowly the intensity of the lights increases and the show begins. Maybe it's Verdi's *Aida*, set in ancient Egypt, whose pomp and splendour match the setting perfectly.

Afterwards, close to midnight, throngs of people – having suspended disbelief for a few memorable hours – disgorge into the night, scrambling not for their chariots but for cars and buses as reality sets in and the ancient entertainments are left behind.

need to know

The Aspendos Opera and Ballet Festival takes place for three to four weeks, starting in mid-June and features Turkish and foreign companies (particularly Russian). Tickets are available in Antalya (around 20YTL/€11), and public buses to Aspendos coincide with performances. Events are held in Aspendos at other times too, and include classical and Turkish music as well as opera and ballet.

21

Every April 30, Amsterdam, a city famed for its easy-going, fun-loving population, manages to crank the party volume a few notches higher in a street party that blasts away for a full 24 hours. Held to celebrate the official birthday of the Dutch monarch, Queen's Day is traditionally the one time each year when the police are forbidden from interfering with any activity, no matter how outrageous; and, of course, it's always a challenge to see where they really draw the line.

Cranking up the Volume on Queen's Day

Stages piled high with huge sound systems take over every available open space, blasting out the beats all day and night – the main stages are on Rembrandtplein and particularly Thorbeckplein, Leidseplein, Nieuwmarkt and Museumplein – and whatever your inclination, you'll find enough beer-chugging, pill-popping and red-hot partying to satisfy the most voracious of appetites. There are only two rules: you must dress as ridiculously as possible, preferably in orange, the Dutch national colour, which adorns virtually every building, boat and body on the day; and you must drink enough beer not to care.

The extensive and picturesque canals are one of the best things about Amsterdam, and Queen's Day makes the most of them, as boating restrictions are lifted (or perhaps just ignored) and everyone goes apeshit on the water – rowboats, barges and old fishing vessels crammed with people, crates of beer and

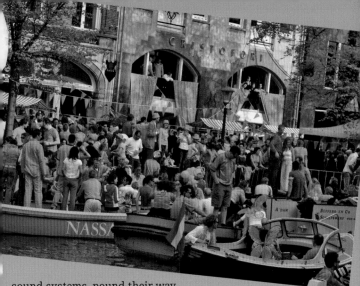

sound systems, pound their way around the canals like entrants in some particularly disorganized aquatic carnival. Your mission is to get on board, as they're a great way to get around – pick one with good tunes and people you like the look of. Or just hang out with everyone else and watch the boats come and go: crowds gather on the larger bridges and canal junctions to cheer on each bizarre vessel – Prinsengracht is a good canal for this, with Reguliersgracht and Prinsengracht a particularly chaotic and enjoyable intersection.

need **to know**

For Queen's Day you need to book accommodation several months in advance. Many bars set up a counter out on the street, and there are Heineken marquees on the edges of Leidseplein, Nieuwmarkt, Rembrandtplein and Dam Square. Amsterdam's main clubs lay on special Queen's Day nights – pick up a copy of the freebie *Amsterdam Weekly* when you arrive to find out what's on.

22

Seeing the Northern Lights, Sweden

They appear as shimmering arcs and waves of light, often blue or green in colour, which seem to sweep their way across the dark skies. During the darkest months of the year, the Northern Lights, or *aurora borealis*, are visible in the night sky all across northern Sweden. Until you see the light displays yourself, it's hard to describe the spectacle in mere words – try to imagine, though, someone waving a fantastically coloured curtain through the air and you've pretty much got the idea.

What makes the Northern Lights so elusive is that it's impossible to predict when they're going to make an appearance. In scientific terms, the displays are caused by solar wind, or streams of particles charged by the sun, hitting the Earth's atmosphere. Different elements produce different colours, for example blue for nitrogen and yellow-green for oxygen.

Undoubtedly, the best place to view these mystical performances is north of the Arctic Circle, where temperatures are well below freezing and the sky is often at its clearest – two conditions that are believed to produce some of the most spectacular sightings.

For the quintessential Northern Lights experience pack a couple of open sandwiches topped with smoked reindeer meat and a thermos of hot coffee to keep out the chill, then take a snow-scooter tour deep into the forests of Swedish Lapland. Park up beside a frozen lake and train your eyes on the sky. Try this between mid-December and mid-January, when there's 24-hour darkness north of the Arctic Circle, and the chances are you won't have to wait long for your celestial fix.

need to know

Sweden's northernmost city, Kiruna, is the best base from which to see the Northern Lights. It can be reached by train or plane from Stockholm. Snow-scooter tours are available from nearby Jukkasjärvi, home to the famous *Icehotel* (℡0980/668 84, ⓦwww.icehotel.com).

23

Burrowing for bargains in Kraków

One of the hazards of hitting Kraków on a Saturday night is that you usually have to spend the next day in bed recovering from the experience. If you're a fan of Sunday-morning flea markets, however, then this is one place where it's well worth dragging yourself out from under the duvet.

Prime target for the city's jumble junkies is Hala Targowa, a semi-covered fruit-and-veg market which is taken over one day a week by stall after stall of old furniture, domestic knick-knacks, objets d'art and – just occasionally – the odd genuine antique. Obsessive collectors can sort through everything from old postcards to used phonecards, or try their luck with the militaria man who carefully lays out his collection on a trestle table and then barks "that's not for sale!" whenever anyone takes

Bargain hunters also abound at the city's other favourite Sunday-morning hangout, the second-hand clothes market on Plac Nowy in the bohemian suburb of Kazimierz, It's a great place to browse, meet friends and tuck into the fat grilled sausages that are permanently on the menu at Poland's markets.

Kraków has a huge student population, always on the lookout for all sorts of bargains. The narrow streets of the city's historic centre are crammed with second-hand bookshops, and not everything they sell is in Polish – Kraków's burgeoning ex-pat population ensures that there's a lot of English-language tomes changing hands as well.

One bookshop that has become a cult location in recent years is Massolit, housed in a rambling creaky floored apartment whose floor-to-ceiling shelves are stuffed with books in English on every aspect of central and eastern European history and culture. Named after the chaotic writers' union described in Russian writer Mikhail Bulgakov's novel *The Master and Margarita*, Massolit also serves Kraków's most delicious home-baked cakes. For anyone weary after a day's bargain hunting, Massolit offers the ideal escape.

need to know
Kraków Tourist Board
@www.krakow.pl
Sunday flea market
(Giełda staroci), Hala
Targowa (Sun 8am–
2pm).
Massolit, ul. Felicianek 4
(Mon–Thurs 10am–8pm,
Sat & Sun 10am–7pm;
@www.massolit.com).

24 Bavarian Bacchanalia:

downing a stein or ten at the

Oktoberfest

The world's largest public festival, the Munich Oktoberfest, kicks off on the third Saturday in September and keeps pumping day after day for a full two weeks. Known locally as the "Wies'n" after the sprawling Theresienwiese park in which it takes place, it was first held to celebrate the wedding of local royalty but is now an unadulterated celebration of beer and Bavarian life, attracting seven million visitors and seeing over four million litres of beer disappear in sixteen days.

At the heart of the festival are fourteen enormous beer tents where boisterous crowds sit at long benches, elbow to elbow, draining one huge litre-capacity glass or "stein" after another. If you're up for annihilation, head to the Hofbrau tent at a weekend, go for the ten-stein challenge and join the thousands of youngbloods braying for beer. If you actually want to remember your time in Munich, or to encounter some real Germans, pitch up midweek and take in two or three of the other beer tents. Whenever and wherever you go, one thing will stay the same – within two steins you'll be laughing with your neighbours like long-lost buddies and banging the table in time with the Oompah bands.

The loudest and busiest time to visit Oktoberfest is the first weekend, when the "Grand Entry of the Oktoberfest Landlords and

Breweries"
starts the whole
thing off as participants attired in Bavarian finery
(lederhosen, basically), decorated carriages, curvaceous
waitresses on horse-drawn floats and booming brass bands from
each of the beer tents parade through town, joined by several
thousand thirsty locals and international partiers.

The local mayor gets things going by tapping the first barrel
of Oktoberfest beer at the park's entrance and declaring
"*Ozapftis*", which means "it's been tapped", but
translates more accurately as, "Why
doesn't everybody get as wasted as
possible in my town for the next
two weeks and don't worry
about the mess because we'll
clear up?" Huge cheers rise
up from the crowd as the
mad dash to the cavernous
beer tents begins.

need to know

Theresienwiese is 1km southwest
of central Munich. The nearest U-
bahn stations are Theresienwiese,
Schwanthalerhohe or Goetheplatz. For
more info, go to ®www.oktoberfest.de.

55

25 Partying all night in Reykjavík

In recent years Reykjavík has earned a reputation for wild revelry that's totally disproportionate with its diminutive size. Spend a summer Friday or Saturday night out here, when there's virtually 24 hours of daylight, and it's easy to see why getting wrecked in Reykjavík has become a rite of passage for Europe's most dedicated hedonists.

Known as the *rúntur*, a Reykjavík pub crawl is precisely what its Icelandic name implies, a "round tour" of the city's drinking establishments. However, a serious night out actually starts at home to help reduce the punitive cost of drinking in Iceland. After several generous vodkas, Reykjavík's well-dressed, well-heeled and well-tipsy take to the streets, albeit somewhat unsteadily, to hit the scene.

As a new face in town, expect to be accosted by revellers dying to know what you think of the local nightlife – they may even invite you to join them. Things change fast on the Reykjavík club scene, though currently the place with the hottest action

is *Oliver*, Laugavegur 20a, whose dancefloor is full of strutting twenty-somethings. Two other favourites are *Hverfisbarinn*, Hverfisgata 20, a buzzy glass-fronted bar that's always packed with beautiful people and *Sirkus*, Klapparstígur 31, a Bohemian club where Björk sometimes DJs.

When the clubs empty at around 3 or 4am the party continues in central Lækjartorg square where those still standing swap notes on how many beers they downed and the night's gossip. Reykjavík is probably the only place in the world where you can go into a club at midnight, just as it's getting dark, party amongst some of Europe's most stylish and fashionable people, and emerge barely a few hours later in broad daylight, wrecked, maybe, but having had a night to remember.

need to know

Icelandair flies to Reykjavík from several European and American cities. Alcohol in Reykjavík is extremely expensive: a beer in a bar costs at least €7, whereas in a club you can expect to pay more in the region of €9.

25

Ultimate
experiences
Europe
miscellany

Languages of Europe

There are 37 indigenous European languages that have more than a million speakers around the world. The five largest are:

Spanish 390m
English 341m
Portuguese 210m
Russian 145m
French 120m

One surprising entry is **Catalan**: it is the largest European language without its own country, and has more speakers (6.7m) than Norwegian (4.6m) and Slovenian (2m) combined.

Yiddish is another oddity, a mixture of German and biblical Hebrew that is spoken only by Jews – chiefly in Eastern Europe and North America – but that, with 3.2m speakers, is more widely understood than, say, Lithuanian (3.1m).

 # Europe's borders

Europe isn't easy to define. In the **north**, Iceland is generally included, as is Svalbard (Norway); in the **south**, the furthest fringes are the Mediterranean islands of Lampedusa (Italy), Malta, Crete (Greece) and Cyprus.

To the **west**, Europe is bordered by the Atlantic Ocean – seemingly straightforward, yet Atlantic archipelagos such as the Azores (Portugal) and Canary Islands (Spain) are politically European, but geographically outside it.

But the **eastern** limit is the trickiest, varying – depending on who you talk to – between the Bosphorus straits, which divide Istanbul, and Russia's Ural Mountains, more than 2000km further east on roughly the same line of longitude as Dubai.

"To understand Europe, you have to be a genius – or French."

Madeleine Albright, US politician

Festival calendar

There are hundreds of European parties, national holidays, parades and festivals. Here are ten of the best:

Festival	When	What happens
Binche Carnival, Belgium	Feb or March	Mardi Gras festival with parades of fancy dressed figures and a food fight with blood oranges.
Las Fallas, Valencia, Spain	March 12–19	Saint's day celebrated with burning *fallas* (effigies) and other pyrotechnics.
St Patrick's Day, Ireland	March 17	There's a parade in Dublin, and drinking everywhere.
Queen's Day, the Netherlands	April 30	When everyone dresses in orange, gets on the water and celebrates the Queen's birthday.
Festa do São João, Porto, Portugal	June 23 and 24	A giant street party – with lots of eating, drinking dancing, fireworks and hitting people over the head – all in honour of the city's patron saint.
Il Palio, Siena, Italy	July 2 and Aug 16	Famous bareback horse races.
Bastille Day, France	July 14	National holiday to celebrate the fall of the Bastille prison and the start of the French Revolution.
Notting Hill, London, UK	Last Sun and Mon of August	Two days of fabulous costumes, parades and sound systems.
Oktoberfest, Munich, Germany	Mid-Sept to early Oct	The world's largest public festival, attracting seven million beer-swilling visitors.
Lewes Bonfire Night, UK	Nov 5	Bonfires and processions in the biggest and weirdest of the celebrations held across the country to celebrate the defeat of the Catholic plotters of 1605.

The Celtic nations

The term "Celtic" traditionally refers to peoples of prehistoric Europe who shared a common culture, and who were in large part conquered and supplanted by the Romans. Today, a fringe of northwestern Europe is still inhabited by people who share an identifiably Celtic culture – expressed in Celtic languages, in a Celtic tradition of ornamental art and sculpture and in Celtic folk music.

Celtic nation	Celtic language	Number of speakers (approximate)
Brittany	Breton (Brezhoneg)	300,000
Cornwall	Cornish (Kernewek)	4,000
Ireland	Irish (Gaeilge)	500,000
Isle of Man	Manx (Ghaelg)	1,700
Scotland	Gaelic (Gàidhlig)	60,000
Wales	Welsh (Cymraeg)	700,000

 # Cities

According to a UN list published in 2006, **Moscow** is the nineteenth most populous city in the world – and the most populous in Europe – with 10,654,000 people, followed by **Paris** (9,820,000), **Istanbul** (9,712,000) and **London** (8,505,000).

"When a man is tired of London, he is tired of life, for there is in London all that life can afford."

Samuel Johnson

"Of the many smells of Athens, two seem to me the most characteristic – garlic and dust."

Evelyn Waugh

Five world-class countryside restaurants

El Bulli, Roses, Spain. Food as theatre in this magnificent setting on a rocky headland on the Costa Brava – expect twenty or more mini-courses, served with a flourish.

Fat Duck, Bray, UK. Combinations of flavours and textures to challenge your palate – and your expectations – in the romantic setting of this Thames-side Berkshire village.

Olivier Roellinger, Cancale, France. Sensational cooking in a small Brittany harbour town, featuring local fish and seafood enhanced with exotic spices.

Oud Sluis, Sluis, Netherlands. This sleepy seaside village near the Belgian border hosts a young, innovative chef quietly working culinary magic.

Schwarzwaldstube, Baiersbronn, Germany. Sublime French cuisine in a sturdily traditional setting, with panoramic views over the Black Forest.

"Fish, to taste right, must swim three times – in water, in butter and in wine."

Polish proverb

 # The Olympic Games

The first Olympic Games took place in 776 BC, in Olympia in Greece. They were held every four years until 393 AD.

In 1612, the English town of **Chipping Campden** staged an "Olimpick Games" sports festival, and has done so regularly since, while nearby **Much Wenlock** launched its "National Olympian Games" in 1850. The French baron Pierre de Coubertin visited Wenlock in 1890, and adopted the idea for the first international Olympic Games of the modern era, which he staged in Athens in 1896.

 # Food

"How can anyone govern a nation that has 246 different kinds of cheese?"

Charles de Gaulle

There are now between 350 and 400 French cheeses.

⏩ Five local foods to try

Dutch herring Best eaten tilting your head back and dangling the fish by its tail into your mouth whole.

Kaffee und kuchen Coffee and cake, a quintessentially Viennese way to pass the time.

Moules frites Mussels with chips – Belgium is renowned for this.

Pizza Served straight from a wood-fired oven, and running with olive oil, in its home town of Naples.

Tapas Go on a tapas crawl in Spain, snacking on each bar's speciality.

"To eat well in England you should have breakfast three times a day."

Somerset Maugham

 # The Orient Express

The Orient Express from Paris to Istanbul is Europe's most famous train. It first ran in 1883. By the 1930s several routings used the name "Orient Express": the original ran from Paris via Strasbourg, Munich, Vienna, Budapest and Bucharest, augmented by the "Simplon Orient Express" via Lausanne, Milan, Venice and Belgrade, and the "Arlberg Orient Express" via Basel, Zurich, Innsbruck, Vienna and Budapest.

Direct Paris–Istanbul service was withdrawn in 1977, although the Orient Express name survives today on the Paris–Vienna overnight sleeper.

10 Ten great European novels

Hardly definitive, but every one a page turner – perfect for those long train journeys across the continent.

War and Peace Tolstoy. Arguably the greatest novel ever written, Tolstoy's masterpiece travels from the gossip-filled rooms of St Petersburg parties to the battlefields of Europe as Napoleon advances.

Madame Bovary Gustave Flaubert. Flaubert's most controversial novel, featuring sex, sleaze and suicide.

Bleak House Charles Dickens. One of Dickens's most ambitious novels, with a complex plot that brilliantly conveys Victorian London and all its ills.

Crime and Punishment Fyodor Dostoyevsky. Dostoyevsky's masterpiece, set in St Petersburg's infamous Haymarket, is a gripping read.

Don Quixote Miguel de Cervantes. Widely regarded as the world's first modern novel, and *the* classic of Spanish literature.

The Leopard Giuseppe di Lampedusa. Sicilian classic, chronicling the dramatic nineteenth-century years of transition from Bourbon to Piedmontese rule from an aristocrat's point of view.

Buddenbrooks Thomas Mann. The story of a late nineteenth-century German family and their gradual disintegration over forty years, but also of the country's transition over this period.

Ulysses James Joyce. An Irish Jew wakes up, goes drinking and wonders if his wife is having an affair. Ripe with classical allusion and visceral crudity, it's at once a challenging read and a feast of great one-liners.

The Trial Franz Kafka. Kafka portrays the darker side of central Europe – the claustrophobia, paranoia and unfathomable bureaucracy – better than anyone else.

Wuthering Heights Emily Brontë. The repercussions of Heathcliff and Cathy's youthful romance scour the bleak Yorkshire Moors in this heady, atmospheric and ingeniously constructed melodrama.

"An artist has no home in Europe except in Paris."
Friedrich Nietzsche

 # Size matters

Europe has some of the smallest sovereign states in the world.

State	Size	Population (approx)
Vatican City	0.5 sq km	900
Monaco	2 sq km	32,000
San Marino	62 sq km	29,000
Liechtenstein	160 sq km	34,000
Malta	316 sq km	400,000
Andorra	466 sq km	71,000
Luxembourg	2600 sq km	470,000

 # Five legendary city-centre hotels

Le Bristol, Paris. The French capital's most opulent hotel, complete with private colonnaded gardens and Gobelins tapestries on the walls.

Danieli, Venice. A magnificent fourteenth-century palazzo with a view over Venice's lagoon, featuring acres of marble, stained glass and Murano chandeliers.

The Dorchester, London. Perhaps London's most famous hotel, a Mayfair landmark since 1931 celebrated for its luxury and super-discreet service.

Grand Hotel Europe, St Petersburg. Not many hotels – even ones to this standard – can boast a visitors' book that includes Queen Elizabeth II, Elton John and Rasputin.

Sacher, Vienna. Spectacular imperial luxury in this hotel dating from 1876, perfectly positioned directly opposite the Opera House.

"Venice is like eating an entire box of chocolate liqueurs in one go."

Truman Capote

13 Eurovision Song contest

The Eurovision Song Contest was started in 1956 as a pan-European TV celebration of popular music, and now attracts up to 500 million viewers worldwide. It's not just the music or even the outlandish costumes that matter: the whole thing is intricately related to European politics. Greece votes for Cyprus but not Turkey, the Balkans back each other and Ireland is the darling of the lot, with a record seven wins – four during the 1990s.

For **Serbia and Montenegro** the choice of representative in 2006, according to former Serbian Prime Minister Zoran Zivkovic, caused "much more excitement…than the death of Slobodan Milosevic". When Montenegrin band No Name were chosen for the second year running, Serbians were appalled, the Montenegrin judge was accused of foul play and the country withdrew from the contest. In May that year Montenegro voted in a referendum for independence from Serbia.

In 2003, the UK received a humiliating **nul points** for the first time. Some blamed the country's involvement in the Iraq war, others that the act, Jemini, sung out of tune.

14 The five best European music festivals

Glastonbury UK. Mud and hippies. The legendary Glastonbury festival has taken place on Michael Eavis's farm most years since 1971.

Roskilde Denmark. The huge rock festival is also famous for holding a naked race on the Saturday – first prize is a ticket to the next year's festival.

Pink Pop The Netherlands. The longest unbroken annual music festival in Europe, for 38 years Pink Pop has been partying in Limburg, south Netherlands.

Exit Serbia. Started in 2001, and held in a dramatic fortress setting in Novi Sad, just north of Belgrade, this festival attracts some world-class bands.

Benicàssim Spain. Featuring big-name bands and heaving dance tents, you can party all night then head to the beach for the day.

The European Union

The European Union (EU) was founded in 1957 as the European Economic Community (EEC, known as the Common Market), with six member states. Since then it has grown to include 27 member states.

Date	Members joining
1957	Belgium, France, West Germany, Italy, Luxembourg, the Netherlands
1973	Denmark, the Republic of Ireland, the UK
1981	Greece
1986	Portugal, Spain
1995	Austria, Finland, Sweden
2004	Cyprus, Czech Republic, Estonia, Hungary, Latvia, Lithuania, Malta, Poland, Slovakia, Slovenia
2007	Bulgaria, Romania

Contrary to popular belief, the flag of the European Union is a fixed design – a circle of twelve gold stars on a blue background. The number of stars has never been related to the number of EU member states.

"The secret of politics? Make a good treaty with Russia."

Otto von Bismarck

 # **Time**

Europe covers several time zones. Iceland, the Irish Republic, the UK and Portugal use GMT ("Greenwich Mean Time"), also known as UTC ("Coordinated Universal Time"). Most of mainland Europe and Scandinavia uses GMT+1. A line of countries from Finland and the Baltic States to Greece and Turkey use GMT+2. Moscow and the western parts of Russia are on GMT+3.

All European countries follow daylight saving between late March and late October – except Iceland, which stays on GMT all year round.

Five unusual European sports

Sport	Played in	What happens
Boules	France	The best-known type of *boules* is *pétanque*; played on a gravel surface, players toss metal balls to land as close as possible to a target wooden ball.
Curling	Scotland	Like bowls on ice: each player slides heavy polished granite stones along a narrow rink, trying to bring the stone to rest in a target area.
Hornussen	Switzerland	An outlandish mixture of golf and baseball: one player launches a puck along a curved track with a long cane; the others try to hit it with large wooden bats before it touches the ground.
Hurling	Republic of Ireland	Hockey on speed: two teams of fifteen players use bats, hands and feet to try and get a small, hard leather ball into a goal.
Korfball	Belgium, the Netherlands	Like egalitarian netball: two teams (of 4 men and 4 women each) try to score baskets against each other.

 # Islands

At 209,000 square kilometres, **Britain** is the largest island in Europe.

Greece has around 1400 islands. About 85 percent of them are uninhabited.

The Frisian islands – around fifty islets strung along the North Sea coast of mainland Europe – are divided into the West Frisian Islands (part of the Netherlands), the East Frisian Islands (Germany) and the North Frisian Islands (Denmark).

Bridges and tunnels

Europe has two of the world's five longest suspension bridges. **The Great Belt Bridge**, part of the link between the islands of Funen and Zealand in Denmark, has a span of 1.624km (second-longest) in its total length of 6.79km, while the **Humber Bridge**, across the Humber estuary in England, has a span of 1.41km (fourth-longest) in its total length of 2.22km.

In Switzerland, two trans-Alpine rail tunnels – the Gotthard and the Lötschberg – are due to be superseded by deeper, straighter replacements, designed to accommodate high-speed trains: in late 2007, the **Lötschberg Base Tunnel** (34.6km) will open, halving journey times between Bern and Brig, while the **Gotthard Base Tunnel** will be the longest rail tunnel in the world when it opens in 2015 (57km), knocking an hour off journey times between Zurich and Milan.

 # Mountains

The highest point in western Europe is **Mont Blanc**, in the French–Italian Alps, at 4807m above sea level. **Mount Elbrus**, in the Russian Caucasus, is higher – at 5642m – but not everyone agrees that it lies in Europe. Europe's highest permanently occupied settlement is **Juf**, a hamlet near St Moritz in Switzerland, at 2126m above sea level.

 # What makes Britain?

The British Isles is a geographical term, referring to an archipelago comprising two large islands (Ireland and Britain), plus around six thousand smaller islands nearby.

The United Kingdom (UK) is a political term, referring to a state comprising the nations of England, Scotland, Wales and Northern Ireland. Fourteen "overseas territories" including Gibraltar, Bermuda and the Falkland Islands are under the sovereignty of the UK.

The Isle of Man, though part of the British Isles, is not in the UK. The **Channel Islands** are neither in the UK nor the British Isles.

22 Europe's five longest rivers

River	Rises in...	Flows through...	Drains into...	Length
Volga	Russia	Russia	Caspian Sea	3690km
Danube	Germany	Germany Austria, Slovakia, Hungary, Croatia, Serbia, Bulgaria, Romania, Moldova, Ukraine	Black Sea	2850km
Dnieper	Russia	Russia, Belarus, Ukraine	Black Sea	2290km
Rhine	Switzerland	Switzerland, Liechtenstein, Austria, Germany, France, Luxembourg, Netherlands	North Sea	1320km
Elbe	Czech Republic	Czech Republic, Germany	North Sea	1091km

23 Beer

Eleven of the twelve countries worldwide with the highest consumption of beer per capita are in Europe. They are (with amount per person per year in litres):

Czech Republic	157	**Belgium**	93
Republic of Ireland	131	**Denmark**	90
Germany	116	**Finland**	85
Australia	*110*	**Luxembourg**	84
Austria	108	**Slovakia**	84
UK	99	**Spain**	84

24 Dracula: Europe's most famous vampire

The Irish novelist Bram Stoker's story of a bloodthirsty nobleman, **Dracula** (published 1897), is fictional – but Stoker loosely based the figure of Count Dracula on Vlad III of Wallachia (1431–76). Vlad's father was known as Dracul ("dragon"), a title passed on as Draculea ("Son of Dracul").

Vlad is reputed to have killed around 150,000 people, mostly by impaling them on sharp poles. Stoker's inspiration for Dracula's vampirism probably came from the tale of the Hungarian Countess Báthory (1560–1614), who – according to legend – tortured and killed thousands of girls before drinking and bathing in their blood.

Stoker placed Dracula's castle in Transylvania, which borders Wallachia in modern Romania. Today Romania promotes the atmospheric Transylvanian fortress of Bran as "Dracula's Castle", though its associations with Vlad are tangential – and resisted by many Romanians.

25 The Basque Country

The **Basque** people have lived in a region of the western Pyrenees, which spans Spain and France, for at least two thousand years. Their language is unique, unrelated to any other language spoken today or known in history.

Three Spanish provinces form an autonomous Basque region known as Euskadi (total population around 2.1 million), where both Basque and Spanish are official languages. Its largest cities are Bilbao and San Sebastián. The region of Navarra is also part of the Basque homeland. The Basque areas in France, including Basse-Navarre, form part of the *département* of Pyrénées Atlantiques.

Ultimate
experiences
Europe
small print

Europe
The complete experience

ROUGH GUIDES – don't just travel

We hope you've been inspired by the experiences in this book. To us, they sum up what makes Europe such an extraordinary and stimulating place to travel. There are 24 other books in the 25 Ultimate experiences series, each conceived to whet your appetite for travel and for everything the world has to offer. As well as covering the globe, the 25s series also includes books on **Journeys, World Food, Adventure Travel, Places to Stay, Ethical Travel, Wildlife Adventures** and **Wonders of the World**.

When you start planning your trip, Rough Guides' new-look guides, maps and phrasebooks are the ultimate companions. For 25 years we've been refining what makes a good guidebook and we now include more colour photos and more information – on average 50% more pages – than any of our competitors. Just look for the sky-blue spines.

Rough Guides don't just travel – we also believe in getting the most out of life without a passport. Since the publication of the bestselling Rough Guides to **The Internet** and **World Music**, we've brought out a wide range of lively and authoritative guides on everything from **Climate Change** to **Hip-Hop**, from **MySpace** to **Film Noir** and from **The Brain** to **The Rolling Stones**.

Publishing information

Rough Guide 25 Ultimate experiences Europe Published May 2007 by Rough Guides Ltd, 80 Strand, London WC2R 0RL
345 Hudson St, 4th Floor, New York, NY 10014, USA
14 Local Shopping Centre, Panchsheel Park, New Delhi 110017, India
Distributed by the Penguin Group
Penguin Books Ltd,
80 Strand, London WC2R 0RL
Penguin Group (USA)
375 Hudson Street, NY 10014, USA
Penguin Group (Australia)
250 Camberwell Road, Camberwell, Victoria 3124, Australia
Penguin Books Canada Ltd,
10 Alcorn Avenue, Toronto, Ontario, Canada M4V 1E4
Penguin Group (NZ)
67 Apollo Drive, Mairangi Bay, Auckland 1310, New Zealand

Printed in China
© Rough Guides 2007
No part of this book may be reproduced in any form without permission from the publisher except for the quotation of brief passages in reviews.
80pp
A catalogue record for this book is available from the British Library
ISBN: 978-1-84353-819-6
The publishers and authors have done their best to ensure the accuracy and currency of all the information in **Rough Guide 25 Ultimate experiences Europe**, however, they can accept no responsibility for any loss, injury, or inconvenience sustained by any traveller as a result of information or advice contained in the guide.

1   3   5   7   9   8   6   4   2

Rough Guide credits

Editor: Alice Park
Design & picture research: Andrew Oliver, Scott Stickland
Cartography: Maxine Repath, Katie Lloyd-Jones

Cover design: Diana Jarvis, Chloë Roberts
Production: Aimee Hampson, Katherine Owers
Proofreader: Sarah Eno

The authors

Jan Dodd (Experience 1) is author of the *Rough Guide to Dordogne and the Lot*. **John Fisher** (Experiences 2, 10) is co-author of Rough Guides to Greece and Athens. **Keith Drew** (Experience 3) is a senior travel editor for Rough Guides and freelance travel journalist. **Lily Hyde** (Experience 4) has travelled extensively and worked as a journalist in Eastern Europe. **Helena Smith** (Experience 5) is a freelance author, editor and photographer. **Martin Dunford** (Experiences 6, 11, 14, 21, 24) is a co-founder of Rough Guides and has authored Rough Guides to Brussels, Rome and Italy. **Matthew Teller** (Experience 7 and Miscellany) is the author of the *Rough Guide to Switzerland* and is co-author of the *Rough Guide to the Italian Lakes*. **Paul Gray** (Experience 8) is co-author of the *Rough Guide to Ireland*. **Brendon Griffin** (Experience 9) has contributed to Rough Guides on Spain and Portugal. **James Proctor** (Experiences 12, 22, 25) is co-author of Rough Guides to Sweden and Iceland. **Jonathan Bousfield** (Experiences 13, 15, 23) is the author of Rough Guides to the Baltic States and Croatia, and co-author of Rough Guides to Austria, Bulgaria and Poland. **Caroline Osborne** (Experience 16) is co-author of the *Rough Guide to Copenhagan*. **Terry Richardson** (Experiences 17, 20) is co-author of the *Rough Guide to Turkey*. **Matthew Hancock** (Experience 18) is co-author of the *Rough Guide to Portugal* and author of *Rough Guide Directions Lisbon*. **Ruth Blackmore** (Experience 19) is a senior travel editor for Rough Guides and co-author of the *Rough Guide to Paris*.

Picture credits

ROUGH GUIDES · ROUGH GUIDES · ROUGH GUIDES · ROUGH GUIDES

New Zealand

Budapest

Thailand

Greece

Punk

ROUGH GUIDES · ROUGH GUIDES

Italy

India

Over 70 reference books and hundreds of travel
guides, maps & phrasebooks that cover the world